Chana Akins is a professor of Psychology and Neuroscience at the University of Kentucky. She loves science, traveling, and nature.

Beth Ann Rice is a professor of Psychology and Neuroscience at Slippery Rock University. She loves teaching, gardening, and birds.

CHANA AKINS AND BETH ANN RICE

A BRAINY BOOK
ABOUT
NEURONS AND BEYOND

AUSTIN MACAULEY PUBLISHERS™

LONDON • CAMBRIDGE • NEW YORK • SHARJAH

Ordering Information
Quantity sales: Special discounts are available on quantity purchases by corporations, associations, and others. For details, contact the publisher at the address below.

Publisher's Cataloging-in-Publication data
Akins, Chana and Rice ,Beth Ann
A Brainy Book about Neurons and Beyond

ISBN 9798889100256 (Paperback)
ISBN 9798889100263 (ePub e-book)

Library of Congress Control Number: 2024911393

www.austinmacauley.com/us

First Published 2024
Austin Macauley Publishers LLC
40 Wall Street, 33rd Floor, Suite 3302
New York, NY 10005
USA

mail-usa@austinmacauley.com
+1 (646) 5125767

This book is dedicated to Maia, Emilia, and Sabrina
Bulger and Abi Osterholm.

This book can be used as a teaching resource and for
outreach initiatives focused on brain education.

Chapter One
What Is Your Brain?

We have over 70 organs in our bodies, like our lungs and heart. Your brain is the control center for all of your organs. This makes your brain one amazing organ! The average human brain weighs about three pounds which is about how much a bag of oranges might weigh. But of course, the brain weighs a little less in babies and younger children. Once the brain reaches about three pounds in weight, it stops growing in size but it continues to change as we grow. Because the brain helps us do just about everything, it has to be organized in a special way. Keep reading and you will see how the brain is organized.

At the bottom of the brain is the brainstem (like the stem of a flower or leaf). The brainstem connects the brain to the spinal cord. The brainstem is super important for basic life functions like breathing, heart rate, and blood pressure.

Brainstem

Your spinal cord is made of a bundle of nerves, like a thick cable that has a bunch of wires in it. The nerves are covered by bones called vertebrae (ver-tuh-bray). The spinal cord starts at the bottom of your brain and runs down the back of your neck down to your tailbone. The brain needs protection too, so it is also covered in bones. You may know these bones as the 'skull'.

A Bit of Trivia: Humans and giraffes have the same number of vertebrae in their necks but giraffes have joints between their bones (like the ones in your arm) that make their necks flexible and rubbery.

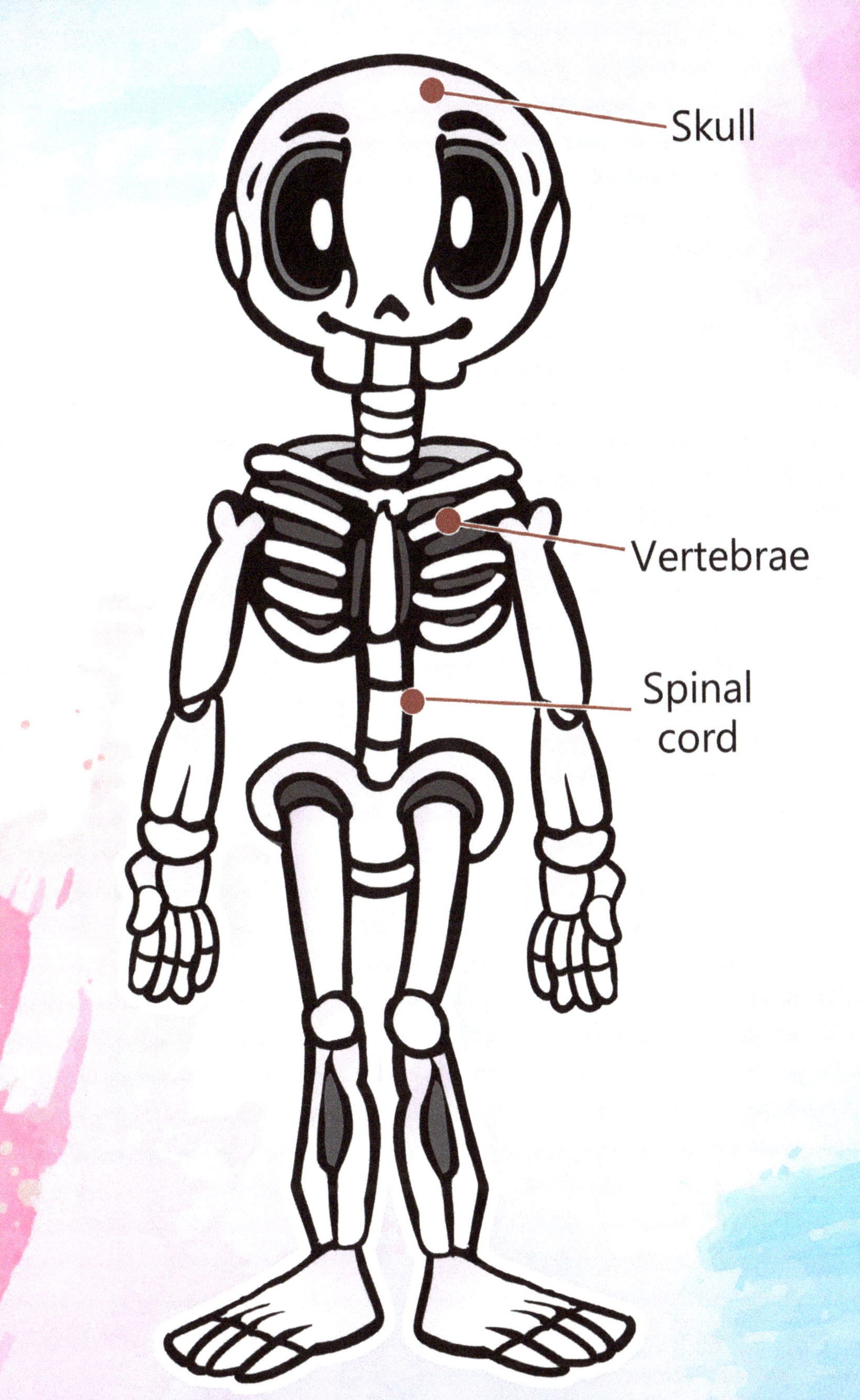

Skull
Vertebrae
Spinal
cord

Chapter Two
What's All That Gray Stuff (Or Is It Pink)?

Inside of our skulls, the brain is more like a pink color because it has so many veins and arteries that carry blood. But outside of the skull, the brain might look more grayish. The gray color of the brain is called "gray matter" and it's the billions of brain cells that give it the gray color. Take a look at a real photo of a brain and see what you think.

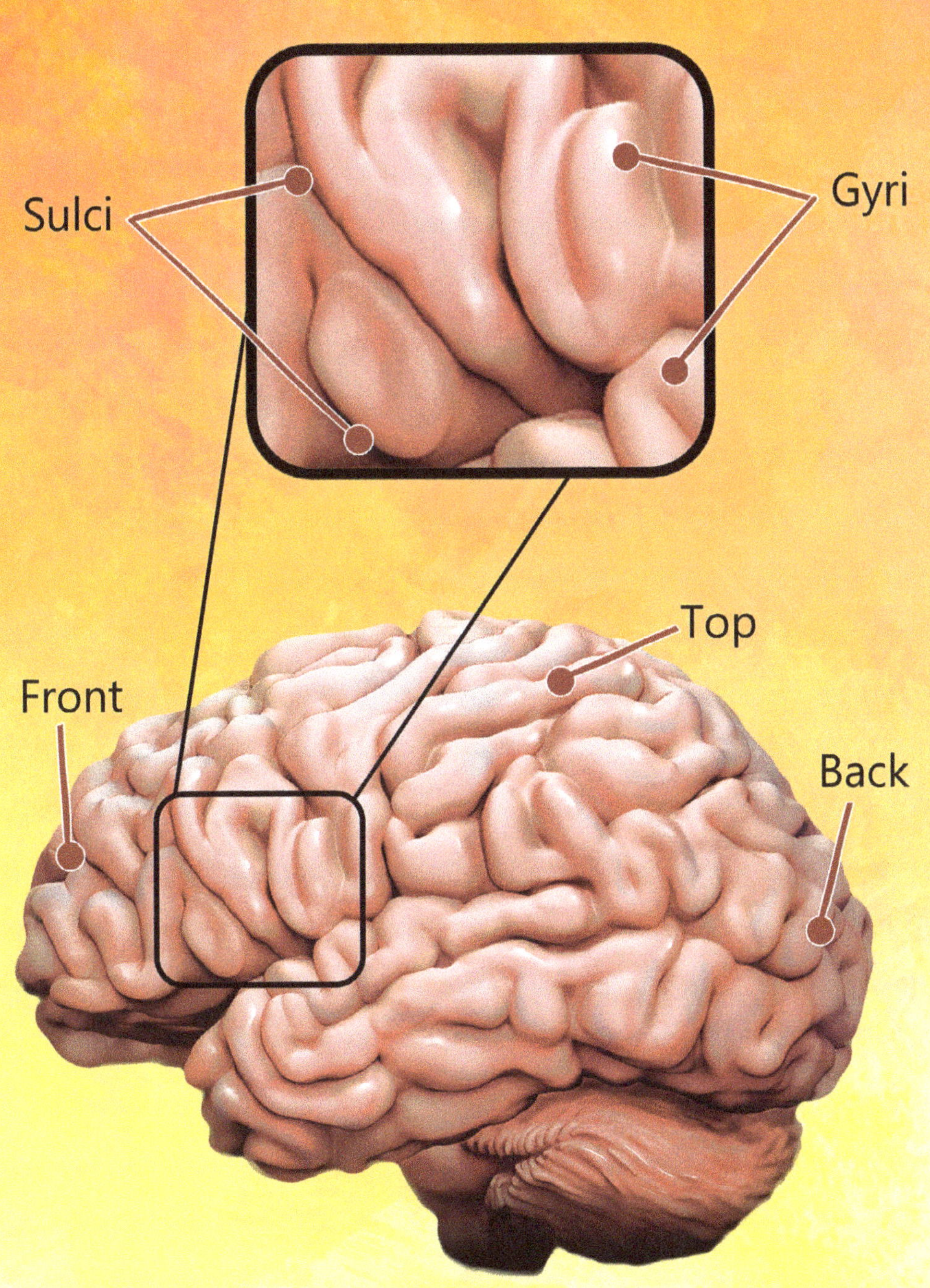

Sulci
Gyri
Top
Front
Back

The outside of the brain is called the cerebrum (suh-ree-brum). The cerebrum has what looks like wrinkles and these wrinkles are what help the brain hold a lot of information.

Activity: If you take a piece of notebook paper and ball it up as tight as you can, you can create a simple paper model of the brain. Let's try it. Go get a piece of paper and ball it up as tight as you can. Now look at your ball of paper. It is smaller than the flat sheet of paper because it is packed, just like the brain. So what is the brain packed with? It is packed with folds or wrinkles just like your paper model. If your paper model were a brain, and you stuck your finger into one of the folds, you would be sticking your finger into a 'sulcus' (suhl-cuss) of the brain. A sulcus is a fold or a groove on the surface of the brain. As you can see from your paper model, there are many grooves that, together, are called 'sulci' (suhl-ki). Now, put your finger on one of the bumps or bulges sticking out between the folds. Now you are touching a 'gyrus' (gy-russ). Bumps on the surface of the brain are called 'gyri' (gy-ri).

A Tale of Two Hemispheres

Sulci are not the biggest grooves in the cerebrum. The biggest grooves in the cerebrum are called 'fissures' (fizz-ers). The largest and deepest fissure is called the 'longitudinal' (lon-ji-toodin-uhl) fissure. This fissure splits the cerebrum into two halves, down the middle of your brain. The cerebrum is like a big globe or 'sphere', but because it has two halves, each half is called a 'hemisphere' (him-is-fear). Hemi, as in hemisphere, means half.

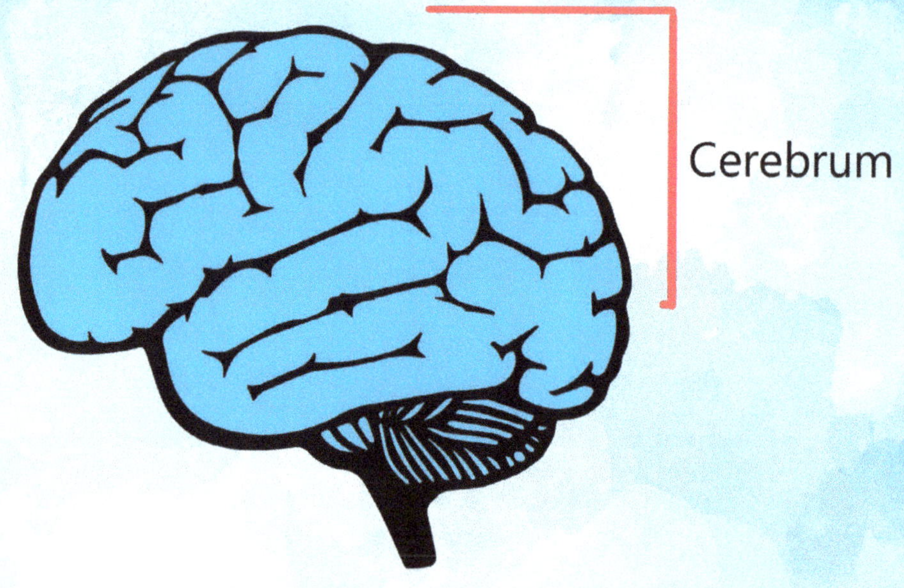

Cerebrum
Longitudinal fissure 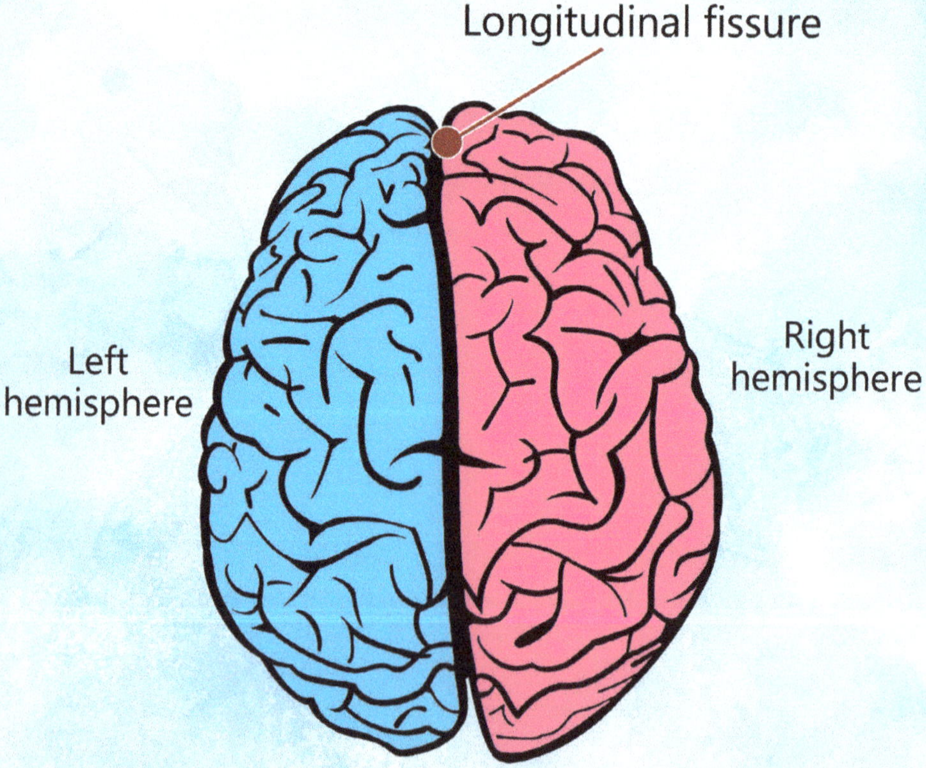
Left hemisphere
Right hemisphere

The longitudinal fissure splits the cerebrum in half but the two halves of the brain still need to talk. The 'corpus callosum' (corpus cuhl-o-sum) allows the two hemispheres (sides) of the brain to talk with each other. Amazingly, the cerebrum's right hemisphere controls the left side of the body. The left half hemisphere controls the right side of your body. For example, if you prefer to write with your right hand, you are right-hand dominant and your left hemisphere is mostly in control of your right hand. If you prefer to write with your left hand, you are left-hand dominant and your right hemisphere is mostly in control of your left hand.

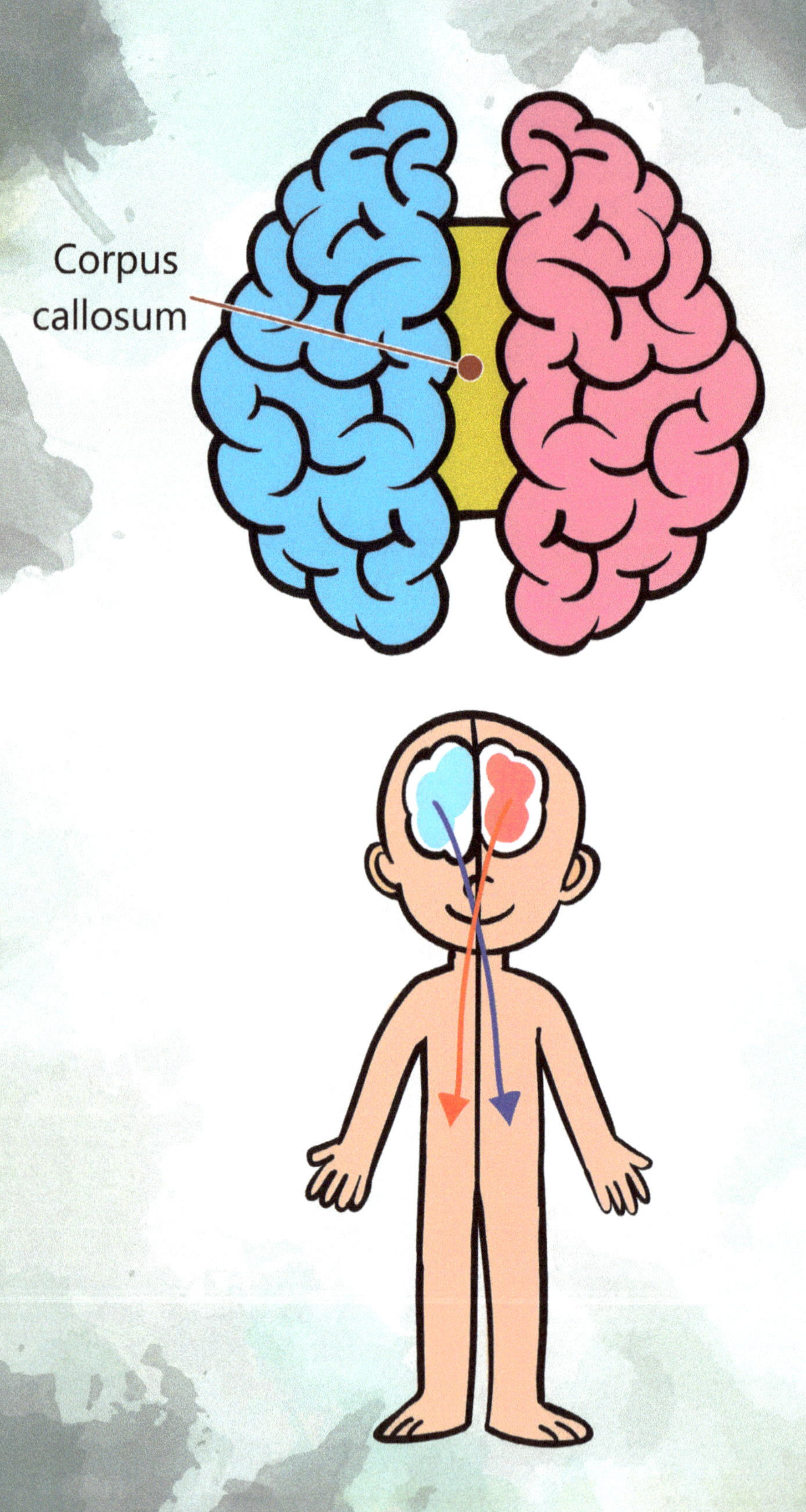

Corpus
callosum

A Bit of Trivia: Most humans are right-hand dominant and fewer are left-hand dominant. There are a rare few that can use both the right and left hand equally. They are called 'ambidextrous' (am-bee-dex-struss).

Activity: If you have a pet or can watch an animal outside, you might be able to see which paw or limb they prefer (although some don't have a preference). If a cat or a dog is playing with a toy or a ball, they may use a certain paw or limb to reach for it or step on it. This is easier to see in a cat or a dog and harder to see in some animals like turtles. But even mice, gerbils, hamsters, and some birds might pick up their food more with one limb or claw than the other. They can be right- or left-limb dominant too.

Wow! At this point, you have learned an awful lot about that gray stuff. But one more important thing about the cerebrum is how it helps us do things. As we talked about earlier, the way the brain is organized is super important. Recall that you have two hemispheres of the cerebrum. Each hemisphere has four lobes.

Activity: One way to think of the lobes is to use your fist as a brain model. Make a fist and you can see what look like lobes of the brain. The bent fingers of your fist are like the frontal (front-uhl) lobe. Your knuckles on top of your fist are like the parietal (per-eye-tuhl) lobe. The thumb of your fist is like your temporal (tim-per-uhl) lobe though it doesn't stick out that far. And last but not least, at the back of your wrist where your wrist bends is like your occipital (ox-ip-it-tuhl) lobe.

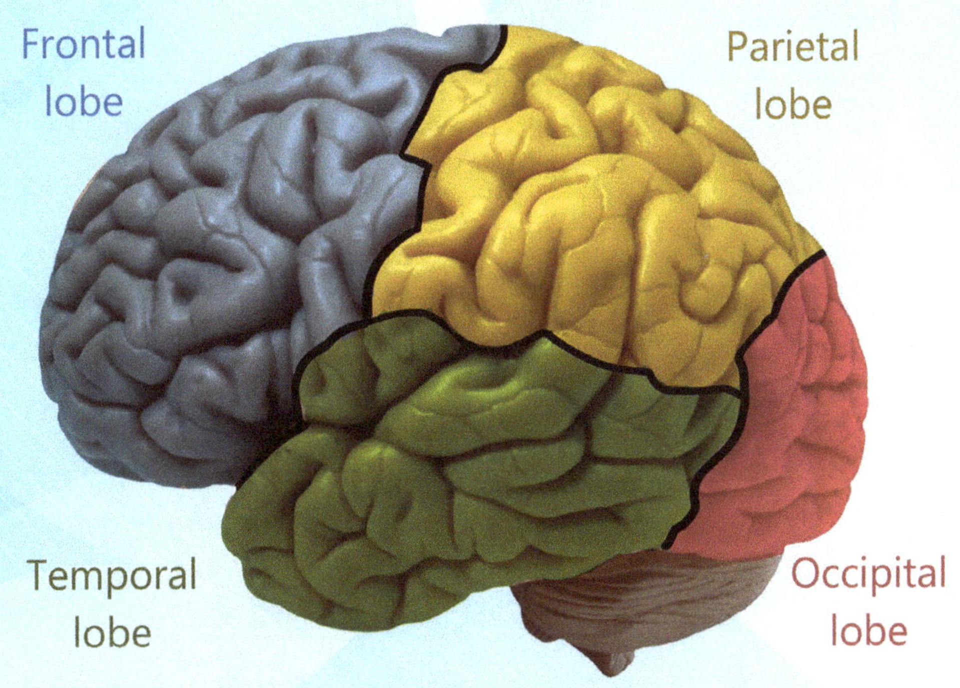

Frontal
lobe
Parietal
lobe
Temporal
lobe
Occipital
lobe

But what does each lobe help us do? The frontal lobe controls our movement. It also helps us to plan, reason, and problem solve. It takes up a lot of space at the front and top of the brain. Just behind the frontal lobe (knuckles at the top of your fist) is the parietal lobe. It helps us to feel touch, pressure, temperature, and pain. If you touch something cold, it is the parietal lobe that tells you it is cold.

If your fist were a small brain, your thumb is just about where the temporal lobe would be located. In the brain, the temporal lobe is located near the ear. That is a big hint that it might be involved in hearing… and it is! And it is also involved in speech and language. The occipital lobe is located at the back of the brain (the back of your wrist of your fist model) and is involved in seeing.

A Bit of Trivia: If you get hit in the back of the head, you might see stars. This is because you probably banged your occipital lobe, which affected your vision and made you "see stars".

Chapter Three
What Is All the Chatter
Inside Your Brain?

The gray matter contains your nerve cells. Nerve cells are called "neurons" (nur-onz). There are 86 billion neurons in the brain, maybe as many as there are stars in the Milky Way. Neurons are tiny in size and difficult to see.

Activity: To see how small a large neuron is, you will need a single strand of human hair and a small piece of paper. Take the strand of hair and hold it against the paper. Look closely at the end of the hair and see if you can see the diameter (the distance across the tip of the hair). A single strand of human hair is about 65–75 microns in diameter. A large neuron is about 100 microns in diameter, so a large neuron is a little bigger round than the size of a single human hair (and 20 times larger than the smallest neurons!).

Neuron
Strand
of
Hair

Neurons do the talking

Neurons are awesome because they are really good at relaying information from one neuron to the next and to parts of the brain and body. If you touch something hot, one neuron picks up the information and sends it to a second neuron. The second neuron sends the information to a third neuron. This last neuron tells your muscles to respond. Your muscles quickly snatch your hand away from the hot object. This is called a reflex because it lets you make a quick response. Then a neuron sends information to the brain that tells you "Ouuuch! That was hot!" Remember that there are billions of neurons in the human body so lots of neurons are working together. They do a lot of talking!

A Bit of Trivia: The average human reaction to touch is about 150 milliseconds. This is about half the time it takes us to blink. Reflexes happen so fast because the information doesn't have to go all the way up to the brain first.

Sensory
neuron
Interneuron
Spinal
cord
Motor
neuron
Muscle contracts

The pupil is the black spot in the center of your eye. The black spot or pupil is actually a hole in the iris. (The iris is the color part of your eyes.) The pupil opens and closes to control the amount of light that goes into the eyes. When the pupil opens more, the black spot gets bigger and it lets more light in. When the pupil closes, the black spot gets smaller and lets in less light. Too much light can damage the eye so the pupils respond to protect against that. The pupils do what is called "the light reflex." You can test this reflex yourself.

Activity: Dim the lights in a room for a few minutes and look at your pupil in the mirror or have someone else look at it. Look at the size of it. If you then turn the lights back on, your pupil should be smaller. The change can happen quickly after the lights are turned back on so have a mirror ready.

Chapter Four
What Does the Brain Do?

Your brain is an amazing organ because it is involved in nearly everything we do, think, and feel. Imagine you are walking down the street and you pass a big row of bushes that have flowers. Suddenly, you get a big whiff of the flowers. At first you start to cough because the smell is so strong but then you notice that it smells nice. A ha! Your nose helped you smell the flowers but your brain told you it was a nice smell. Whether it is smelling, tasting, touching, hearing, or seeing something, the brain receives this information and tries to make sense of it. In this chapter, we will look more closely at each of our five senses and see how this information goes to the brain.

See
Taste
Smell
Hear
Touch

Take A Whiff

Inside the nose, we have millions of neurons called olfactory neurons. These olfactory neurons have tiny hair cells that capture odors from the air and send the information to your brain. But first, the odor makes a pit stop at the olfactory bulb that sends odor information to other parts of the brain, including parts that involve memory and emotion. This connection of smell, memory and emotion could be why when you smell Thanksgiving dinner being cooked, it reminds you of family gatherings.

A Bit of Trivia: Dogs have millions more olfactory cells than we have. This might explain why their sense of smell is much better than ours. Dogs can sniff out a lot of things such as some diseases and even when humans are stressed. And because dogs can pick up scents for more than a mile away, they are often used as trackers by police and rescue workers.

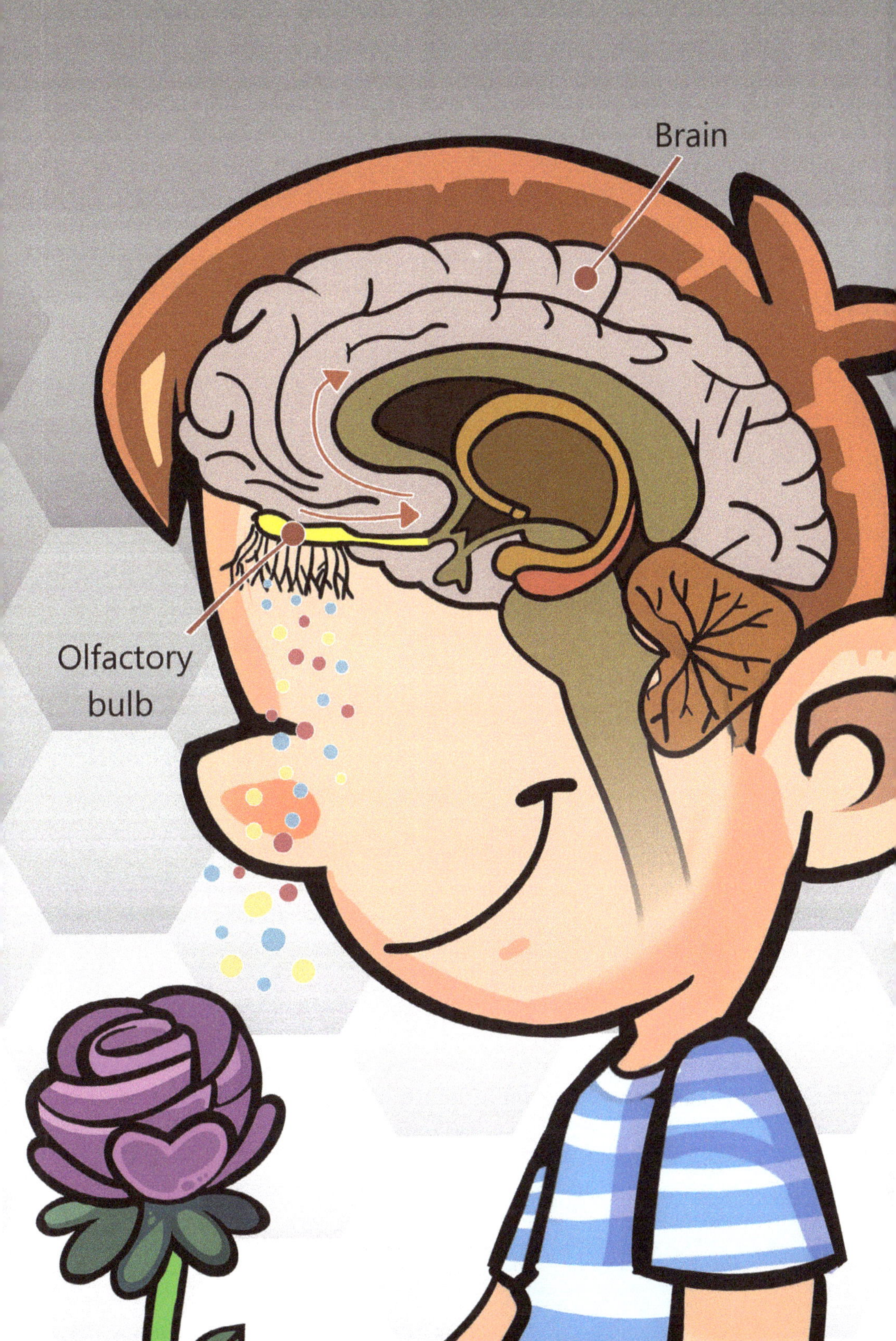

Brain
Olfactory
bulb

Yum and Yuck!

The tongue is used to detect the taste of things but it's the brain that tells you how something tastes. The tiny bumps on your tongue are called taste buds. You have about 10,000 taste buds on your tongue and there are taste buds for salty, sweet, sour, and bitter tastes. Recently, researchers discovered a fifth taste called "umami" (ooo-mom-mie). Umami is a savory taste that some people say tastes like a yummy meat broth. Each taste bud has many neurons. These neurons send taste information to the brain.

A Bit of Trivia: Cats do not have taste buds for "sweet" so next time you want to give your cat a treat, make it savory. Though they might still enjoy cake crumbs if the cake was made with milk and butter.

Taste buds

Drop It Like It's Hot

Within your skin are lots of neurons. These neurons gather touch information about temperature, pain, and pressure and send it to the spinal cord. Touch information is sent to the spinal cord before it goes to the brain so that you can react quickly without thinking about it (remember the reflex in Chapter 3?). It also goes to the brain where we get our understanding of what something feels like. Which part of the brain tells us what something feels like? The part of the brain that tells you what something feels like when you touch it is the parietal lobe (remember the fist in Chapter 2?).

Ouch

Can You Hear Me Now?

Sound is made of vibrations in the air or sound waves. Your ears help you to hear sounds in the form of sound waves. But sound waves have to travel to a special part of the brain to help us make sense of them. First, those big (or little) flaps on each side of your head (Pinna), funnel sound waves into your ear canal. The ear canal is where you might find some ear wax. Inside the ear canal, sound waves hit the ear drum. The eardrum vibrates and sets a series of three bones inside the ear into motion. The motion from these bones causes fluid to slosh around inside of a snail-like structure, about the size of a pea, called the cochlea (co-clee-uh). The sloshing of the fluid in the cochlea activates neurons and those neurons send the sound wave information to the brain. Which part of the brain receives this sound information? Sound information is received by the temporal lobe, which if you recall, is located next to your ear.

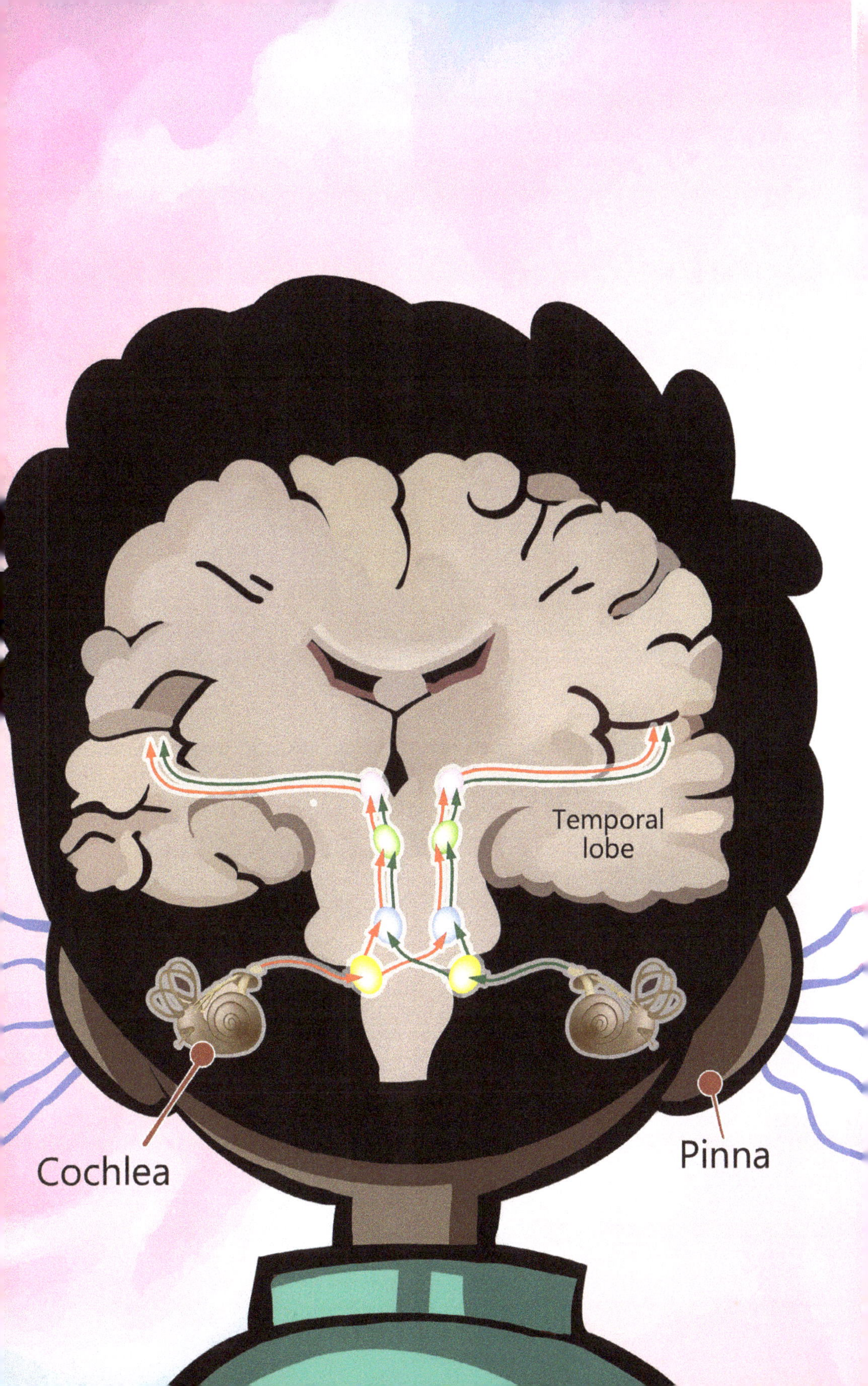

Temporal lobe
Cochlea
Pinna

Activity: You might need a few friends or family members for this one. The game Marco Polo requires the use of our hearing to localize sound. Most of the time, it is played in a swimming pool but it can also be played in an enclosed space, like a backyard. Players must stay inside the pool or yard. One person is "it" (named Marco). The person who is "it" shouts, "Marco!" and the other players shout, "Polo!" and Marco has to tag one of the players that shouted Polo. The tricky part is that Marco has to be blindfolded or have their eyes closed and can only use sound to find and tag the other players who are shouting "Polo!" No peeking Marco.

Out of Sight, Out of Mind

How do we see? Light bounces off of everything you see and it goes into the eye through the cornea (cor-nee-a), the clear outer covering of the eye. It then travels through a hole in the iris, the pupil. The iris has muscles that control the size of the pupil and it is where your eye color is located. Recall, we talked about the pupil as the small black dot in the middle of the eye that changes size based on light or darkness. Behind the pupil is the lens. The lens changes shape to focus the light onto the back of the eye. The back of the eye is the retina (re-tin-uh). The retina has special neurons called "photoreceptors". When the photoreceptors are activated by light, they send visual information to the brain. Which part of the brain interprets this light information? It is the occipital lobe, all the way in the back of your head (Remember the fist in Chapter 2?)

Retina
Cornea
Pupil
Lens
Photoreceptors
Cone
Rod

A Bit of Trivia: Newborn babies don't produce tears. They make crying sounds, but the tears don't start flowing until they are between four and 13 weeks old.

The retina is only about as thick as a postage stamp but it has about 130 million photoreceptors. There are two types of photoreceptors called rods and cones. They are called rods and cones because their shape resembles either a rod or a cone. We use rods mostly in dim light or in the dark. They do not help us see color very well. They help us see in shades of grey. We are pretty much colorblind in dim light. We use cones to see color and mostly in bright light. Cones do not work very well without light. Cones are found in the center of the retina but rods are outside of the center.

Activity: Here's how you can test where rods and cones are located in your eyes. Go outside or look out of a window up at the sky on a night when there are stars in the sky. If you are trying to look at a dim or faint star, you might not see it well if you look straight at it (because you are using the cones in the center of the retina). But if you try turning your head and looking from the side, you might see the dim star better because you are using your rods on the outer part of the retina. And rods help us see better in dim light.

We hope you learned a lot about the brain. There is more to the brain than the eyes can see on the surface and it does a lot of things. If you have to go back and read or practice activities in this book, it's okay. It's a lot to learn about so take your time, read this book over and over again, and most of all, HAVE FUN LEARNING!

THE END